Jaen Carlyle Graham

Songs, measures, metrical lines

Jaen Carlyle Graham

Songs, measures, metrical lines

ISBN/EAN: 9783741112652

Manufactured in Europe, USA, Canada, Australia, Japa

Cover: Foto ©Angelika Wolter / pixelio.de

Manufactured and distributed by brebook publishing software (www.brebook.com)

Jaen Carlyle Graham

Songs, measures, metrical lines

SONGS, MEASURES

METRICAL LINES

MEASURES
METRICAL LINES

BY

JEAN CARLYLE GRAHAM

LONDON
KEGAN PAUL, TRENCH, TRÜBNER & CO., LTD.
PATERNOSTER HOUSE
1893

DEDICATION

To One, whose sage, judicial course
   Of 'damning with faint praise,'
So fired my soul and nerved my force,
   That I, self-scorning, raise

This poetasting cairn to mark
   The spot where I lay prone,
And writhed and rhymed in outer dark,
   Verse-draggled, fierce, and lone!

CONTENTS

PART I.—SONGS

	PAGE
The Rose so Sweet	3
When Meads in May. (*Set to music of R. Schumann*)	4
'The Night cometh'	5
'The Night, it departeth—departeth!'	7
May Song	8
Lulu	10
There's a bonnie bit o' green grass	11
Erinnerung. (*Set to music of R. Schumann*)	15
Song of the Clock	16
When Loris laughs	17
Scots Song	19
Sleep	21
To my Tyrant	22
Song	23
Christmas Bells	24
Wedded. (*Set to music of R. Schumann*)	26

Golden Wedding Song .　　.　.
Janet .　.　.　.　.　.　.
From East to West. (*Set to music of R. Schumann*)
Träumerei. (*Set to music of R. Schumann*)
A Song of the Ides of March　　　　.

PART II.—MEASURES

Silth .　.　.　.
The Victorian Statesman　　　.
The Hours .　.　.　.　.
The Strife of the Seasons. (4 *Pieces*) .
To Mary .　.　.　.
After Sundown .　.　.
Of Love. (2 *Pieces*) .　　.
To our beloved Princess
Pricks　.　.　.
The Passing of Spring .
The Dying Year .　　.　.　.
Death　.　.　　.　.
Lifeless Leaves .　　.　.　.
A Rondeau .　.　　.　.　.
By the Abject Lover .　.　　.
Night and Day .　　.　　.
A Scots Ballad　　　　.　　　.

PART III.—METRICAL LINES

	PAGE
'No Flowers—'	75
The Secret of the Lord	80
To J. R. W.	83
At Morfa. March 1890	85
In Remembrance	91
Athletics	94
Three Chapters from the Book of the Wisdom of Jacob Tew. (*In Deeshire dialect*)	95
In the Waiting-Room of an Eye Hospital	109
Blue Hyacinths	116
The First Kiss	120
'Work—while it is Day'	123

I

SONGS

THE ROSE SO SWEET

The rose so sweet may wound rash hands,
   Heigh ho! beware the thorn.
Her proud pink face your love demands,
   Heigh ho! the heart all torn.

She decks herself in gems of dew,
   Heigh ho! on a summer's morn.
The sparkles may mean tears for you,
   Heigh ho! poor youth forlorn.

She folds her perfume petalled close,
   Heigh ho! on a summer's morn.
The scent may prove a poison dose,
   Heigh ho! that you'd ne'er been born

She flaunts her branches in your face,
   Heigh ho! on a breezy morn.
But stay—the frost will come a-pace,
   Heigh ho! poor rose, all shorn.

WHEN MEADS IN MAY

I

When meads in May with flowers are gay
    And woods with song are glad,
When cooing doves do woo their loves,
    A maiden wanders sad.
      Ah, hapless fate! alone to wait!
Her joys are fled, her love lies dead.

II

When meadows low are white with snow
    And woods are dumb and sad,
When mateless doves do mourn their loves,
    The maid alone is glad.
      Ah, happy fate! in death to mate!
Her woes are fled. The maid lies dead.

'THE NIGHT COMETH'

I

Stay, lovely, loving, saffron light!
    Enfold yon drowsy hills,
Infuse with lucent lymph yon brooding height
    Whence flow the nascent rills.

II

Stay, crawling shades of purple hue!
    Dim army of sad Night!
Nor silent scale yon stony rampire blue
    In fell, resistless fight.

III

Stay, wan, far-glancing eyes of eve!
    Vex not the sun's last gaze;
Faint Day hath yet some passing sighs to heave,
    Toward Death his step delays.

IV

Ah! stay with us, glamour of Prime!
    Love's vesture of gold!
Ah! fly from us, shadow of Time!
    Black, numbing, and cold.

V

Ineffable Eyes of an endless, immutable Night!
Far-set in blue spans of mind-baffling, unscaleable
    height—
  Ah! leave us our day,
    With its tranquil and homely glow,
  Our little bright sphere,
    That we see and feel and know!

VI

Dust atoms that dance on our Sun's gold arc
May vanish and perish,—alone, in the Dark.

'THE NIGHT, IT DEPARTETH,—DEPARTETH!'

I

A SILENCE, as the moment after death—
A silence like a hurt, a sudden pang—
Then, blackness where the faint and quivering breath
Wakes terror of the void from which it sprang.

II

Sun, moon, and stars extinct? We dare not moan.
All hidden life, e'en sense of suffering, gone.
A dim, blank agony of dark,—still,—lone—
Then, with a shivering sigh, awakes the dawn.

III

Wan, chill, as from a vigil, peers the world.
A throb of thankfulness for peril past!
Clear, pearly light steals on—soft mists unfurled—
Birds chirp their orison—
           Day! Day! at last!

MAY SONG

I

To dewy meadows, from whose sheen
Balm-bearing zephyrs perfume glean,
    Away, sweet maids, go play! away!
    Beneath the dappled sky.   'Tis May!

II

The cowslip bells do ring the hour,
The bees do sip from flower to flower.
    Away, sweet maids, away, away!
    Amid the blossoms vie.   'Tis May!

III

The cuckoo chants in bosky bower,
The hedgelings at his plainsong cower.
    Away, sweet maids, away, away!
    Adown the lanes swift hie.   'Tis May!

IV

The blackbird pipes, his love to woo;
The cushat calls his 'poor-poor-doo.'
    Away, sweet maids, away, away!
    To tuneful woods swift fly.   'Tis May!

MAY SONG

V

A daisy chain and hawthorn crown
Sets queen milk-white or queen nut-brown.
Away, sweet maids, to reign, away!
'Neath budding shades, go, lie,—'tis May!

LULU

I

In the glowing summer weather
Bees and I sipped sweets together
'Neath the blue, 'mid honey-heather.
                Lulu! Lulu! Lu!

II

Springing o'er the tufted moss,
Hand in hand, the moor across,
Love lent life a glamour gloss.
                Lulu! Lulu! Lu!

III

Heaven seemed then so near to me.
Now—is there a heaven? Ah me!
Love and faith are fled with thee,
                Lulu! Lulu! Lu!

IV

Chill and dank and blind, I stray
Thro' the clinging mist and grey
O'er the lone moor, lost, to-day.
                Lulu! Lulu! Lu!

THERE'S A BONNIE BIT O' GREEN GRASS

I

There's a bonnie bit o' green grass
    Set round wi' gran' grey trees,
O' gowd I 'd gie a wheen, lass,
    Gin I micht win ower seas,
An' lay me doon an' dream, lass,
    Licht-hearted an' at ease.

II

It 's mony an' mony a day, lass,
    Sin there I set me doon
And suppit curds an' whey, lass,
    Wi' a crackit auld horn spoon,
When we were dune wi' play, lass,
    Ae balmy day in June.

III

The leddy-lilies white, lass,
    In raws, a' starry-crowned,
Did glower wi' eyes sae bricht, lass,
    A' ring'd wi' crimson round,
And in the westlan' licht, lass,
    Did scent the vera ground.

IV

Frae cowslips' yellow frocks, lass,
    We sucked the hinny dew,
And blew the fairies' clocks, lass,
    Whaur dandelions grew;
'Remember me's' and stocks, lass,
    We twined wi' pansies blue.

V

And gowan chains sae grand, lass,
    We hung aboot oor necks.
Nae leddies in the land, lass,
    Wi' braws and boos and becks
Were hauf sae fine and grand, lass,
    As you an' me in 'checks'!

VI

An' oh! d'ye mind the craws, lass,
    Their nests o' hazel twigs,
Their parlymints an' laws, lass,
    Black goons and braw grey wigs,
Abune oor heids their caws, lass,
    Their skreighs, and doited rigs!

VII

An' aye the cushy-doos, lass,
    Ayont the Cardross woods
Gied sorrow-laden coos, lass,
    When they had tint their broods.
Ah! 'poor-poor-cushy-doos,' lass,
    Aye gies me waefu' moods.

VIII

Hech! you an' me were ten, lass,
    An' noo we're forty-three—
Hout! a' the warld may ken, lass—
    'Deed, a' the warld may see!
I carena' hauf a prin, lass—
    I'm auld, an' sae are ye.

IX

Through a' life's trials an' waes, lass,
    When fate and fortune glower,
Thae joys o' youthfu' days, lass,
    Are mair than royal dower.
Ay—they were happy days, lass :
    I live them ower an' ower.

X

I'm richer than a' queens, lass,
    For nane can rob frae me
The life-long treasured scenes, lass,
    That nane but me can see !
An'—a' the loss that's been, lass,
    I'll fin' Abune, may-be.

ERINNERUNG

(Set to R. Schumann's music)

Ah! sweet and true, my lost love,
 The hours when we were wed,
Their sweetness, ever new, love,
 Will last till life has fled—
Till life itself has fled.

Though lonely now I wander,
 A pilgrim old and sad,
Those hours are mine for ever,
 I live them and am glad—

Till in our blest Home yonder
We two again are wed.

SONG OF THE CLOCK

I

TIC-TAC. Tic-tac.
Hours are born, hours die.
Tic-tac. Tic-tac.
Hopes are born, hopes fly.

II

Tic-tac. Tic-tac.
Maidens bold, maids shy.
Tic-tac. Tic-tac.
All alike, all vie.

III

Tic-tac. Tic-tac.
Men love, you and I.
Tic-tac. Tic-tac.
All alike, none knows why!

IV

Tic-tac. Tic-tac.
Joys come, joys fly.
Tic-tac. Tic-tac.
Men are born, men die.

WHEN LORIS LAUGHS

I
When Loris laughs, the birds forbear
Their chirps and trills, too well aware
The listening woods their notes can spare
    When Loris laughs.

II
The listening woods their leaves unfold
The music-laden air to hold,
The sun flecks bars and rests of gold,
    When Loris laughs.

III
The little brooks their tinkling hush,
The whirling eddies softly gush,
And lap the stones that stay their rush,
    When Loris laughs.

IV
The crisp fern fronds uncurl their heads,
And creep from out their rocky beds
To hearken where the echo spreads,
    When Loris laughs.

V

The lilies droop their faces fair,
They scarce the load of sweets can bear
That burdens all the perfumed air,
              When Loris laughs.

VI

The meadows deck themselves with light,
The daisies spread their fingers white,
And ope their golden eyes more bright,
              When Loris laughs.

VII

The skies are dyed a deeper blue,
The hills in purple clad anew,
The whole earth wears a roseate hue,
              When Loris laughs.

SCOTS SONG

I

Come, steek the yett, my dawtie,
    Come, sit ye doun, my dear :
I 'll sing ye o' a bridal,
    But whase, ye maunna speer.

II

'Twas 'tween the mirk an' dawning,
    Ae morn in London toun,
Her bridal braws were buskit,
    Nae silks, nor satin goun.

III

The bonnie bride was buskit
    In braverie fu' grand :
Her een like diamonds shinin',
    The purest in the land ;

IV

Her lip wi' smiles a' glintin',
    Her cheek wi' luve a' red,
Her heid set round with honour
    Tae crown the man she wed.

V

She's crown'd her man with honour,
    For he had tint his ain;
She's twined him wi' her true luve,
    For he stood a' his lane.

VI

She's faced his faes fu' dauntless—
    His faes were a' within;
She's bucklered him, this brave lass,
    Wi' her prood scorn o' sin.

VII

Sae, tak' ye tent, my dawtie,
    Sae, tak' ye tent, my dear,
When ithers brag of heroes
    An' mak' a muckle steer,

VIII

Just tell them o' this guid wife
    That's picked her man frae glaur;
For she's gien him her troth-plight
    For gude, nae mair than waur.

SLEEP

(Set to music by H. A. J. Campbell)

COME, come, mist-veiled Sleep!
Steal to me gently and close my tired eyes,
Lay thy cool fingers upon my hot brow,
Chant me sweet music in accents like sighs,
Hush me with lullabies tender and low,
Whisper them softer and softer, till thou
Lap me in silence delicious and deep—
Silence unstirred by a breath. Ah! now—
　Come, come, soft-footed Sleep!

Bear me aloft through the darkening skies
For ever away from the Night where I weep,
Up to the Day where the light never dies,
　Come, come, God's messenger, Sleep!

TO MY TYRANT

(Set to music by H. A. J. Campbell)

My love, my love, so fair, so true,
Sweet tyrant with the eyes flower-blue,
She holds me prisoned, oh! so fast,
With golden chains about me cast.

With chains of gold as light as air,
Wrought of her wavy sun-tinged hair,
And forged with kisses from her lips
And magic of her finger-tips.

From this, my charmed captivity,
I would not, if I could, go free,
But pray her bonds may hold me fast
As long as life and love may last.

SONG

(Set to R. Schumann's music)

LIFE's fresh spring has passed for aye :
Now 'neath summer's fiery ray,
    Weary and faint,
    With mournful plaint,
Onward we toil in glare of Day.

Come, sweet Night, with cooling wing,
Waft us to everlasting Spring.

CHRISTMAS BELLS

I

TOLL, bells! The hours are flying.
Toll, bells! The year's a-dying.
    Strait and low
    On bed of snow
His weary frame is quiet lying.

II

Chime, bells! God's hours are flying.
Chime, bells! Man's rest's a-nighing.
    Under the snow
    The seedlings grow—
The angel reapers their scythes are plying.

III

Ring, bells! Sad hours are flying.
Ring, bells! For care's a-dying.
    Over the snow,
    Solemn and slow,
Heavenly voices of Peace are crying.

IV

Peal, bells! The hours are flying.
Peal, bells! New Year's a-hieing,
   Over the snow
   With rosy glow,
And fragrant breezes of Spring are sighing.

WEDDED

(Set as a duet to R. Schumann's music)

For evermore, ah! love, for evermore.
Ah! blessed vows that seal me thine!
For evermore, my love, for evermore!
Ah! blessed vows that seal thee mine.

To float along Life's tranquil stream
Together, in a blissful dream.
For evermore to love!   Ah! nevermore
From thee to part—not e'en in Death—

    For Love Divine
    Is mine and thine,
And God hath made us one.

For evermore, for evermore, we two are one.

GOLDEN WEDDING SONG

I

ONCE upon a time, love,
  When you and I were young, love,
  We set our lives to rhyme, love,
  Ourselves a living song, love.

II

We woo, we two;
We coo, be true.
We kiss! no bliss
Like this, I wis.
Love darts, love smarts,
Love parts—break hearts!
We sever for ever—
We sever? ah, never!
Fair weather, together;
Foul weather, together
We two still woo,
We two are true.

III

And now has come a time, love,
When you and I are old, love,
Our lives, still set to rhyme, love,
Accord like harps of gold, love.

JANET

Janet, soft and round and rosy,
Janet, sweet as any posy,
Little roguish, dimpled maiden,
Quaint and fresh, with graces laden.

By your simple, bird-like art
You have nestled in my heart;
There you flutter, chirrup, chatter,
Making it go pitter-patter.

If at three you have the power
Thus to charm at every hour,
What, alas! will hap to me
When your years count six times three!

What, alas! But so that you
To your childish self be true,
You be winsome, fresh, and sweet,
I, your slave, it is most meet.

Witching Janet! play and dance,
I must love, whate'er bechance:
Give your baby charms full sway—
I'm yours, for ever and a day!

FROM EAST TO WEST

(Set to R. Schumann's music)

THOUGH far from thee, dear love, I wander
  O'er pulsing waves that throb and surge,
The moon that silvers thy nest yonder
  On me sheds light from ocean's verge.

    I tell to her my story
    Of fears, of hopes, of love.
I fire my soul with dreams of glory
That I may win for thee, my dove,
      Safe in thy nest,
      In thy soft nest,
      'Neath her sweet light
         At rest.

TRÄUMEREI

(Set to R. Schumann's music)

I

WHEN all the loyal stars are lapt
In sombrous sapphire, dreaming of the regnant Moon;
    When Earth, in lucent veil enwrapt,
Lies one hushed moment ere she greet the Dawn in June;

II

    Midsummer elvish fancies flaunt
Adown the perfumed airs that fret the flowers;
    They wanton rouse, delude, and taunt
The lover, drowsing thro' the fever'd hours.

III

    'Hist! Lute-notes of thy maiden true,
In summer sweetness—
        List! With her the dulcet stream
    Tunes madrigals—Awake! and woo!
Fond lover, wake!'—
    The music faints. Alas, alas! 'Twas but a dream.

A SONG OF THE IDES OF MARCH

(*At Apia Bay*, 1889)

I

THROUGH the long weeks the rough sea-dogs had growled on the chain,
Chafing and snarling, shut in by the reefs from the main,
Watching a bone of contention that neither might grasp,
Panting and heaving defiance with each sullen gasp.
Sons of the Fatherland, sighing for home in one breath,
Dooming their rivals, the next, to confusion and death.
Yankees, cool-headed, outraged, and enraged—for a wonder—
Hurling deep curses amid the Pacific's surf-thunder.
Silently lay on her leash the slim British sleuth-hound,
Blinking, but ready for action, if need should be found.
Low on the shore crouched Mataafa among his armed braves,
Marking the foe as he swung to his doom on the waves.

Duty?—For sure it is duty.—Say why we were
    there?—
Orders from headquarters!—See the black storm in
    the air!
Look to the moorings, strike topmast! Its fiercest
    we'll dare.
German, American, Briton, defiantly glare.

II

Man's puny wrath smouldered red in the narrow-
    necked bay,
March saw the sparks, called the winds, and rose
    joyous to play,
Spurred his white coursers from far in the caves of
    the sea,
Harked on his rabble-rout, roaring and prancing in
    glee.
Sheets of black rain flapped and flew on the boisterous
    blast,
Glad to be free from the sky's gloomy wrappings at
    last,
Breakers rushed on and crashed, tossing their foam-
    crests on high,
Billows long-rolling, with mountainous joy, passed
    them by.
Higher and louder and wilder and faster the fun—

March and his rough-riders, see the mad races they
 run !
Ramp o'er the breakwater, clear the jagged reefs at a
 bound !
Ho ! to the goal ! clear the way ! sweep triumphantly
 round !

III

March, with the unloving eyes of a crystal-clear blue !
March, with the loose-floating locks of the daffodil
 hue !
March, with his mutinous swagger, his conqueror
 smiles !
March, with his flower-broidered mantle that hides
 his black wiles !
Clarion-tongued offspring of tranquil, dumb Grand-
 father Time !
Turbulent nurseling of tempest, mad playmate of
 gales !
Roystering rider on hurricanes ! Malefic mime !
Jester for Death to the music of dying men's wails !

IV

Tell of him, ocean deeps ! Toss up his castaway toys!
Float up the fragments and scraps of once exquisite
 joys,

Flung to thy keeping when tired of his frenzy of play,
Battered and tattered and shattered—his sports of a day.
Chant of him, mermaidens! Sing of the brave ships he threw,
Tortive and splintered and torpent, to rot in your caves.
Show us the trash—'treasure-trove of the sea'—once a crew—
Flotsam of souls that drifts dank on the rhythm of the waves.

V

March on his courser swift-winged rides at full racing speed:
Flower-broidered mantle? gold locks? who is this on the steed?
Grey, grinning skull, see the blots in dark sockets!— Blue eyes?
Grim, stark, and dumb, a winged dragon bestriding, who flies?

VI

Frolic and scamper, Death's playmates! whirl on without check!
Rain, wave, and hurricane! Race it with *him* neck to neck!

VII

Ware! helpless rivals that glare each at each in the
   dark!
Cease your vain menaces! Who heeds them?—Ware!
   Silence! Hark!

VIII

Clangs of wild harmonies,—
Clashes of discord, and wails,—
Strains of Death's war-song are fitfully borne on the
   gales.
Cries of the drowning,
Deep groans of despair—then a rush—
Down to the coral cells, dumb, in the eloquent
   hush.

IX

Broke with a terrible grandeur the dawning of day,
Strove with the blackness to add to the dread of the
   fray,
Saw the brave war-ships wild rolling, in anguish sore
   pressed,
Gulfed in the billows or flung on each horrible crest.

X

Hark! 'tis a cheer that rings glad o'er the howl of the blast.
Brother, God speed! Hurrah! Cheer! though this breath be our last!
Cheer them on gaily, hurrah on the brink of the grave!
Cheer! as your kinsmen win past, slowly breasting the wave.
Fire! ye child heroes! blaze out like God's stars in the gloom.
Heed not Death's war-chant that menaces, reck not of doom!
Panting, half-conscious, nigh mad with the agonised strain!—
Cheer! Three times three! The *Calliope* rides on the main!

XI

Hail, glad Columbia! Shed tears of an extasate pride,
Mother of heroes! yon cheer wakes an echo worldwide.
Teuton! American! Briton! Samoan! ye are one—
Brothers of Death's mighty Conqueror, kin to God's Son!

XII

Kaisers and Presidents, Statesmen ! proud breakers of
   Law !
Ye that cram souls, living souls, in Ambition's wide
   maw !
Look to your disciplined dare-devils dashed on the reef,
Dead at their duty—your work—as thieves watching
   a thief !

XIII

Chroniclers! prating of 'epochs in wide-world-history,'
Diplomats ! mincing at Congresses, framing word
   mystery :
Say, was the matter an adequate reason for strife ?
Say, was possession worth more than a fellow-man's
   life !
' Blessings of Civilisation ! '—you suavely reply.
' Progress of Dominant Races ! '—oh ! spare us the
   cry.
' Cession !—nay, *Purchase* from Natives ! ' (a handful
   of beans !).
' Flag of Protection, of course ! ' ' Annexation ! ' (that
   means ?).
Burglars may answer. *They* dress it in slang like the
   rest.
Stealing is banal—to euphuize gives it a zest.

Ruffle it gallantly! bravos of Civilisation!
Bend with politeness, and deal a fair share to each
    nation!

XIV

Pirates, speak truth!   You'll shame none but the
    coiner of lies.
Fight!   Snatch the booty!   Sail off with it!   Plant!
    Colonise!
Fittest!   Survive!   'Tis the law of this world.
                                      For the next—?
Answer, dead watchdogs that toss in yon harbour,
    surf-vexed.

XV

Man! with your visions supreme of a world-ringèd
    rule.
Man! with your pitiful strivings, poor passionate
    fool!
Man! with your gold-gorgèd monsters to work your
    mad will.
Man! with mechanical brain-births to breathe by your
    skill.
Greedy for gewgaws that stud the earth's girdle of
    seas,
Battling to keep them, promulgating laws and decrees.

Grabbing (the strong from the weak) what ?—some
   ocean-washed stones :
Calling them Empires and Kingdoms, Dominions and
   Thrones !
Mock at him, Winds ! from your realm of which none
   knows the bound.
Laugh at him, Storms ! as ye roll your majestical
   round.
Breathe, Love seraphic ! pure breath from yon vast,
   awful Arch !
Breathe on these puppets—limp, dead—on this Ides
   of March !

II

MEASURES

SILTH

A SONNET

THE burdened year rolls down the hill of Fame.
Oblivion's sullen caldron, at the base,
Wrinkles a leaden grin the plunge to erase,
And settles o'er the slimy load of shame
Life's shards and rags, too mean and soiled to name.
Would God that they had passed and left no trace,
There, on the height before her brazen face
Whose hundred tongues clang out the praise and blame!
See! on the plains! the iron-clad peoples smile
Lip-smiles: croon 'Peace,' and lull the infant year,
Raise mailèd hands of warning or of guile
To still Fame's trumpet-clamour from his ear!
The babe *will* wake, *will* scale that steep, full-grown,
And load him with the silth Old Year has strown.

Xmas 1892-93.

THE VICTORIAN STATESMAN

I

He guards Her realm with heart and eye and hand,
    That she, enthronèd there
    Secure, serene, and fair,
May reign, a wise Queen, o'er a peaceful land.

II

That he, her servant, loyal may alway be,
    His every deed and thought
    By Honour's self is taught;
And he, her friend, not slave; in bonds, yet free.

THE HOURS

My Soul hath twice twelve servants at her beck,
Who, noiseless, speed their way with wingèd feet.
Some bear the flowers wherewith my Soul may deck
Time's altar,—some, with step, alas! too fleet,
Flash sun-rays on her path that dazzling fleck,
Then fade,—and some bring clouds and rain and sleet
(True servants they, though grief their pace may
    check),—
And some whose sad-hued pinions, lagging, beat
The heavy air, raise storms that well-nigh wreck
Her peace,—and others still, breathe scorching heat
'Neath which she faints.
                Flower-laden hours! so sweet,
Oh, stay your perfumed pinions at her feet!
Sun-flashing hours, with rays so bright, so fleet,
Ah! fly not till my Soul her rest doth meet!

THE STRIFE OF THE SEASONS

I.—SPRING

COLD Winter, clad in hard and glittering mail,
With starry, frost-gemmed shield before his breast,
Rears proud his jaggèd helm and snowy crest,
And tosses wild his locks of rattling hail.
He yells a war-cry, wails a weird death-wail,
Then spurs his storm-steed, lays ice-lance in rest
To meet his jocund foe—and falls sore pressed,
To die. 'Gainst lusty Spring he fights to fail.
Gay, leafen-vested Spring! whose battle gear
Is fairy wrought, whose casque is primrose dight;
Whose shield, of tasselled saplings wove; whose
    spear,
A bar of sunbeams tipped with fiery light.
Birds flute Spring's war-song to enchant the ear,
'Tis winter's dirge, and love-lay of the year.

II.—SUMMER

Bold Madam Summer, with her love-lit eyes,
And cheeks and lips of milk and roses red,
Comes gliding o'er the meads with perfumed sighs
To seek the rustic swain she wills to wed.
Capricious Spring lies hid in covert deep :
He dreads to wear his conqueror's flow'ry yoke,
So hies him to the woods, and feigns to sleep,
And dons a mist-veil for a magic cloak.
'Tis all in vain! His fate steals on apace :
She bends the branches with warm finger-tips,
She leans o'er him the blossom of her face,
Breathes off his mist-veil, lays to his her lips.
He wakes, he smiles, he frowns and weeps in play,
And, chained with wreaths, is captive led away.

III.—AUTUMN

FAIR, bounteous Autumn, from her mother-heart,
To Summer, dying of Love's poisoned dart,
Brings store of joys to glad her waning days.
She clothes the hills and vales in golden haze;
To deck bruised petals, dusty leaves, parch'd meads,
She nightly borrows from King Frost his beads,
And strings with them the wonders of her dyes—
Gay chromic tints that each with other vies !—
With luscious juice the rounding fruit she teems;
With gentle tears she swells the cooling streams;
And when the harvest moon's red lustre beams,
Lulls Summer's pains with poppies till she dreams :
Then gently from her rival's nerveless hold
Her sceptre takes, and dons her crown of gold.

IV.—WINTER

Her blessèd task of giving nigh its close,
Crowned Autumn, oldened by her lavish sway,
In silent sadness seeks well-earned repose,
And leaves her tuneless realm to sad Decay.
Her sheaves of golden grain are garnered high,
Brown nuts and ruddy apples, russet pears,
And earthen-coated roots laid safely by,
For sombre heaven a boding aspect wears.
Then Winter, from afar, sends warning moan
And message-whispers to the waiting woods ;
The leaves fall shuddering down, the branches groan,
And o'er the sodden fields a dank fog broods.
And now, in rushing triumph Winter comes,
And Autumn to his stormy might succumbs.

TO MARY

A SONNET

THE living beauties my dear maid doth wear
No human voice but lacketh tune to sing!
To her the cherished sprites of nature bring
Their treasured grace, as to a casket rare.
The sunbeams twine the mazes of her hair;
The zephyrs flush her cheek with perfumed wing,
And, sporting with her, teach her foot their spring;
Rose-elves to paint her curvèd lips do dare;
The sea its sapphire hides in her fringed eyes;
The clouds lend softness to her rounded limbs.
Her mind with fresh-fallen snow in whiteness vies,
No stain of earth its dazzling lustre dims.
And Love, to sum this hoard of beauteous health,
In her soft bosom stores his matchless wealth!

AFTER SUNDOWN

A SONNET

THE listening air is cool and clear and still,
The opal sky reflects the sun's last flush,
Translucid clouds are poised in softest hush,
The birds have ceased their evening anthems shrill,
A holy silence broods o'er vale and hill—
Save where the torrent on its seaward rush
Doth chafe the rocks, and round and o'er them gush
In clamouring haste its mission to fulfil.
So sinks fair Day to rest by labour won :
May we, too, when our tallied task is done,
In memory stay, though we have ceased to breathe,
And love-suffusèd peacefulness bequeathe :
That harassed toilers, 'mid earth's rush and strife,
May thus foretaste the calm of Endless Life.

OF LOVE

TWO SONNETS

I

How deep the mystery of Woman's love!
As ivy wreathes the elm, whose rugged rind
It clasps and hides 'neath myriad tendrils kind—
The rougher rind, the closer laced above
The ever green and glossy sheath,—so love
In Woman's mystic and unreasoning mind
Doth clothe with grace her hidden idol, shrined,
Unworthy tho' it be. Not so Man's love!
His idol must be moulded fair to see,
Set high for all his fellows to adore ;
The fairer and the farther off it be,
The greater his desire, his ardour more!
But Man's or Woman's love is one in this—
The while it stays, 'tis blinding, 'wildering bliss.

II

THE while Love stays!—Ah! wherefore doth Love fly?
The nestlings flutter off 'neath heaven's free dome
When all too strait they deem their moss-walled home.
So, Love from narrowing bounds will roving hie.
'Tis all in vain his wings to clip, or tie
A silken band to blind him! He will roam
From walls too strait to be his lasting home,
From nest where rival winglings with him vie!
Who fain would house Dan Cupid needs beware
No mean nor envious wight usurp his seat:
The heart that homes him must be dwelling fair,
Of royal space and fragrance, as is meet!
The lordly urchin will be All or None:
So, mortals, see to it! lest ye be undone.

TO OUR BELOVED PRINCESS

A SONNET. JAN. 1892

TAKE comfort, break not, tender mother heart!
See, all the mothers in the land do weep
With thee, that thou thy son must lay to sleep
Where no soft kiss of thine will bid him start
Awake one morn to bravely do his part
'Mid men, for Man ; on perilous height and steep
To guard the flag of Britain, and to keep
Her beacons lit with flame from his royal heart.
Ah, gentle nurse! Years since, when thou didst tend
Another couch, we watched with thee, we prayed—
Death fled—unsatisfied. Then we did bend
In adoration of the hand that stayed
Death's grasp. We blindly ask for life—Ah me!
God grants, denies ;—We trust. We cannot see.

PRICKS

A SONNET

THE wounds that sword doth gape and talon tear,
That may be healed and hid by timely craft—
E'en tho' they slay—win fame. The barbèd shaft
In battle flown, that fleshes aim, doth bear
Proud plumes the archer and his mark may wear.
E'en coward Poison, with its deadly draught,
Blends rest from care with pain, when fully quaffed.
Plague's dial points to health, Fire clears the air.
But cruellest ills are those Fame never sings,
Too deep for Pity's gentle dews to heal:
Fanged sneer, steeled word, the spur of scorn—their sting's
Unseen! Large, tender hearts that bleed to feel
Vicarious stabs, small daily pricks will kill,
If hands well-loved do choose the spot with skill.

THE PASSING OF SPRING

A BALLADE

THE tender turquoise-tinted sky,
The filmy clouds that float and play,
And toss their soft white arms on high
To hide the sun's hot gaze and lay
Cool shadows on the meadows gay,
Where cattle crop the sweet new grass,
And mother sheep call lambs that stray—
    Say,—Summer comes!
          Spring goes, alas!

Skylarks that shrill and trill, and ply
Undaunted wings, and soar their way
And breast air-tides, till dazzled eye
Blinks till they drop and cease their lay;
Lapwings that flap and wheel and say
'Pee-wit, keep-hid!' then cunning pass
The nest and sideways swing and sway—
    Cry,—Summer comes!
          Spring goes, alas!

Swallows that circle, dart, and hie
From comb to eave with insect prey
To gaping broods that huddled lie
Safe-nested in hid homes of clay ;
Flute-throated blackbirds, throstles grey,
The chiff-chaff with his sharp ' chiss-chass,'
Wrens, tits, and warblers—all the day
    Sing,—Summer comes !
        Spring goes, alas !

L'ENVOI

All living things—the wreaths of May,
The trees, the scented new-mown hay,
Pinks, blue-bells, lilies, perfumes crass—
    Breathe,—Summer comes !
        Spring goes, alas !

THE DYING YEAR

The cold winds wail thy dirge, thou dying Year!
The rain is falling fast from yon dark cloud
That veils the winter moon whose radiance clear
Of late had wrapped, as in a silvered shroud,
The straight, still outlines of the land. Now, drear
And bare, with tossing limbs, the trees are bowed,
And, rending, groan above thy hidden bier.
The darkness is awake, and memories crowd
And rustle in the dusk. Like ghosts appear
Joys, griefs, despairs, and hopes; ambitions proud,
And grovelling meannesses. Each sight of fear,
Each sound of cheer thy past hath known. Loves
    vowed,
Loves lost, Hates hissed, Wrongs wreaked,—all, all
    are here:
The twelve-act passion-drama of a year.

DEATH

Death keeps Life's gate.
                    Why need we fear,
Or hold Death to be aught but dear
To men or any living thing!
He stands, cloud-robed, with folded wing,
And patient waits from year to year.

He turns Life's key when we draw near,
When Time our straying footstep brings
Home to our Father's House of Cheer.
                Death keeps Life's gate.

Death hath no voice that mortal ear
Need shrink nor agonise to hear!
He calls us as an angel sings,
In silver tones whose echo rings
From Heaven to Earth most sweet and clear!
                Death keeps Life's gate.

LIFELESS LEAVES

A TINY bunch of lifeless, faded leaves—
   Lifeless, are they?
When now from them a living memory weaves
   A web to-day,
In living colours, of a bygone scene!
   Of purple heath
On dark hillside;—of tree-clad isle, whose green
   The lake beneath
Has prisoned in its still and glassy deeps;—
   Of white wreathed mist
That floats and curls up giddy mountain steeps;—
   Of crags cloud-kissed
That dare the storms in silent hardihood;—
   Of o'er them all
The soft grey billows of the sky that brood
   And threat to fall
In tears o'er isle-gemmed, crag-engirdled lake!
   Lifeless, are they?
When fraught with living power that seems to make
   This winter's day

Put on the semblance of a day long-past,
              Where those leaves grew
In Summer's green, unknowing 'twas their last.
              So, thus anew,
By these dry leaflets do we breathe the still,
              [1]Gale-scented air,
Behold the loveliness of loch and hill,
              And feel, as there,
That e'en God's clouds and rains fulfil His will,
              And are most fair.

[1] Gale = bog-myrtle.

A RONDEAU

                When I am dead,
For ever dream of me
As one whose love still nestles close to thee.
A day-long guardian of thy words and ways,
My spirit will be set, to see thee raise
A temple of good deeds for men to see.
A hiding-place of solace may'st thou be,
A tower of strength to which the weak may flee;
And all who know thee trust thee in the days
                When I am dead.
Yea, know and trust—but never love like me;
For none may love my love, save only He
Who gave him to me that my soul might praise
The Giver,—full of lowly, sweet amaze
At my own bliss. Ah! love, think thus of me
                When I am dead.

BY THE ABJECT LOVER

A SONNET

Ah! would I were that dimple on thy chin!
Ah! would I were that rose upon thy lip!
I'm jealous of these sweets that thou dost sip,
That gossamer that floats athwart thy skin.
Could I but be the jewel that doth pin
Those wavy locks that wanton from its clip,
That thou mightst touch me with thy finger-tip,
I'd ask no more! So, near thee I might win,
I'd even be the leather of thy shoe
That thy light tread might thrill me thro' and thro',
Until I wore to death in serving thee!
I care not what I be, so thine I be!
And thou, sweet witch, that know'st thy power
    too well—
Each day for me thou weav'st anew some spell.

NIGHT AND DAY

I

SEE from the silvered edge of yon dark hill
In silent majesty the moon doth rise;
The paling stars, abashed, do shrink and thrill,
And haste in lustrous veils to hide their eyes,
Where feathery floating clouds do sail the skies:
Her pearly glory to the Night doth lend
A glamour soft, whose beauty doth the Day's
    transcend.

II

The dazzling, sceptred Day is hard and proud;
Beneath his sway the earth doth sweat and toil;
His wakeful choirs with myriad voices loud
Enclang his praises in a rhythmic coil;
His liveried hosts' gay hues each other foil;
Th' enslavèd globe he drags in glittering chain
Along the Oval vast where Sol, his lord, doth reign.

III

Oh! work-compelling, truth-revealing Day!
Oh! rest-enticing, secret-shrining Night!
Alike in this, that ye His Word obey
That called ye out of chaos, and made Light
That ye in awful splendour be bedight!
In mystic stillness—in harmonic roar—
Alike ye call on us the Maker to adore.

A SCOTS BALLAD

I

THE easterly haar creepit in frae the sea,
    The Year was a meenute auld,
When Bell Kirkmichael cam' ower the muir—
    The nicht was mirk and cauld.

II

She happit her wean wi' her checkit plaid,
    She happit it close and warm,
Her face glints white in the mirk-black nicht,
    And dour like an oncome o' storm.

III

My Leddy Dhunwhassel sits high in the Ha'
    In a bleeze o' licht like day;
My Lord her son, wi' his weel-tochered bride,
    Was keepin' his Hogmanay.

IV

The Leddy she rose frae her tamboured chair,
  The clock's on the stroke, quo' she,
Fling wide the doors, let the New Year in,
  Let the Auld Year flee, quo' she.

V

They 've flung the Ha' doors wide to the wa',
  The easterly haar creepit in,
The Auld Year passed wi' a grewsome sigh,
  It fled wi' its burden o' sin.

VI

They 've flung the Ha' doors wide to the wa':
  Oh! wha comes here? cried she.
What blythe first-footer comes in wi' the Year
  Tae bring me my arles? cried she.

VII

I 've brocht ye an arles, my Leddy sae blythe,
  —The voice was hoarse, wi' a girr—
A braw lass-bairn o' your ain red blude,
  God mete as ye mete tae her.

VIII

An' Bell Kirkmichael cam' ben the Ha'
   In the bleeze o' licht like day,
She laid the wean at the Leddy's foot,
   And, oh! there was dool an' wae!

IX

She rose and she look't on the prood young bride:
   Eh! bride, but ye're bonnie to see.
For a' ye're kirkit bride to yer Lord,
   Ye'll ne'er lo'e yer man like me.

X

She turned and she look't on the braw young Earl,
   He gied her look for look;
Tho' ne'er a word went betwixt them twa,
   It was read like a prented book.

XI

Oh! fare-ye-weel, my Lord sae fause—
   She said it a' wi' her e'e:
Oh! whaur ye gaun, my lass sae wud?
   Tho' never a word spake he.

XII

Then, dumb and white, like a wraith she sped
    Frae the Ha' wi' its bleezin' licht,
Oot-bye in the cauld and the easterly haar,
    Awa' in the black, mirk nicht.

XIII

I 've waukit ower mony a winter nicht,
    An' I fain wad sleep, cried she.
There 's a cauld, blae loch on the brown muirside
    Will mak' a saft bed tae me.

XIV

And the puir wee wean at the Leddy's foot,
    It waukit and blinkit its e'en,
And smile't in the Leddy's awesome face—
    It was warm and blythe and bien.

XV

The Leddy she happit the wean tae her breist:
    Eh! bairn, ye 've a weird tae dree.
My son, ye maun keep this lass frae skaith
    To your dyin' day, quo' she.

XVI

Her son gaed doun on his silken knee,
    And swore by his fair name tint
Tae guard the bairn o' shame frae skaith
    Thro' Fortune's glower or glint.

XVII

The stately bride, she stept to his side:
    My Lord, your hand, quo' she.
You 'll guard your word. I 'll speer nae mair
    O' this ill ye hae wrocht tae me.

XVIII

This New-Year arles o' yon puir lost lass
    Sall bide in oor hame, quo' she;
For there's nane in a' this warld maun threep
    She lo'ed my man like me.

III

METRICAL LINES

'NO FLOWERS—'

I

When this earth-dwelling of my soul
  Stays void and still, and poor and lone,
Oh! deck it not, thus overthrown,
  With floral alms, the wonted dole.

II

Though love for my fled spirit glow
  Unlessened as of old, when met
By answering warmth that, mingled, set
  A halo on the homestead low,—

III

Leave it to mother-earthen care
  To smooth with tender, verdant palm;
Her tendril fingers, strong and calm,
  Will clasp the clay with garlands rare.

IV

With living garlands! Glad to be
   Alive, tho' living on my grave.
The shining leaves God's light will lave,
   And daisies stare and smile to see

V

The pranks the dancing sunbeams play.
   Let bees suck honey there from flowers
That hoard the sweets from gracious showers;
   Let butterflies, the livelong day,

VI

Flicker and sport around the spot.
   But bring no living joys to fade
And die for me! God hath not made
   These gladsome things for so mean lot.

VII

This clay-wrought frame was hardly worth
   The tribute of one violet's life—
E'en when it held a spirit rife
   With thought and passion from the birth.

VIII

God's human flowers are not so pure,
    Are scarce more precious, not so fair
As these He paints with pride and care
    To dress His earth. — And why immure

IX

Such free, fresh beings in this cell—
    A cell from which all light has fled?
Let savage warrior's serfs, who bled
    To grace his death, by thousands yell;

X

Let Orient widowed girls lie bound
    And shrieking writhe upon the pyre
With their lost lords, a prey to fire—
    Whom sensual, gloating priests surround:—

XI

But you—these victims that ye bring
    So meek and dumb, they do not cry
A protest at their doom. Then why
    Their glowing limbs in bonds enring?

XII

Think ye to pleasure Heav'n's ripe grain?
   Or is it for the Reaper-God
Ye leave them drooping on the sod?
   Or, do you seek to stanch the vein

XIII

Of bleeding grief by this your task
   Of binding perfumed crown and cross
As solace?   From your sense of loss
   Why raise a bower where Death can lurk

XIV

And revel 'mid the sweet new life
   That stirs the bosom of the earth
Whence your dear treasure-hoard of worth—
   Be 't husband, lover, child, or wife—

XV

Has passed to Paradise, to tend
   The flowers that never droop nor die?
Ah! ye that weave the wreaths to die,
   And o'er them, black with gloom, who bend—

XVI

Ye that kneel low and weep, look up !
 Nor shower salt tears o'er my void home.
Look up ! Look up to yon starred Dome,
 Where, am'ranth-crowned, I with the Bridegroom sup.

THE SECRET OF THE LORD

I

GRAND four-square tower of Law, erect upon the shore
Of Life's unquiet sea! With lofty wide-set door,
Rock-founded stands a refuge and a home for all
Who drift or steer or toss beneath its strong-built wall.

II

Then why need fussy man heap brittle laws on laws
To shift with every murmuring breeze like unbound
    straws?
Why seek to fence, with paper screens, from Life's
    rough blast
Himself and storm-beat fellow-wanderers in the Vast?

III

High Beacon-tower of Law, with quenchless lamp
    ablaze,
And myriad search-lights flashing o'er Life's darkest
    ways!
Fire crownèd stands, a warning and a guide to all
Who lag or grope or run beneath its crystal wall.

IV

Then wherefore burn a flickering rushlight on mud
    floor,
And seek to scan by its poor spark Life's mystic lore,
Or fondly hope to find the outlet of Life's maze,
In darkest night, by one poor dim horn-lantern's rays?

V

God's moral laws are Ten—wise, equal, broad, and
    plain :
The man who tries to live outside them lives in vain.

VI

Wise :—on the rock of perfect Truth and Knowledge
    based,
That fallen man, through them, to highest type be
    raised.

VII

Equal :—for man and fellow-man are one, tho' two.
By 'Shalts,' no less than 'Shalt nots,' Man God's will
    must do.

VIII

Broad :—for the Love that made them has no mea-
    sured bound.
Plain :—that His feeble, wandering sheep may all be
    found.

IX

God's moral laws are Ten. The Christ who kept
    them knew
Their height and depth, their length and breadth,—He
    only knew.
He kept them here on earth, that men might keep
    them too,
And by Obedience win to Knowledge of The True.

X

Love Man. Love God. Love all God's creatures.
    Know God's works.
Beneath the broadening train of this fair sequence
    lurks
The Secret in a Secret—flawless gem, long-sought!
The pearl of perfect bliss which gold has never bought.

TO J. R. W.

I

Two decades has our friendship seen.
To thee, a time of added joys and partaged woes :
      To me, has been
Most poor, but richest of my life.

II

Now, at another's open door
We stand, hand-claspt, to go two ways—alas !—
      who knows?—
      For evermore,
But for God's heart, with pity rife.

III

And I, for brightening of thy way,
Leave in thy hand a little book of English song,
      Whose music may
Soothe thee to rest, or rouse to strife.

IV

If from its ring some echoes wake
Of true notes, sweet or sad, we have together sung,
    I pray thee make
Such tones a chord to link to mine thy life.

AT MORFA

MARCH 1890

I

' THERE's twenty horses in the mine ! '
' Poor beasts !—What help for it ?—'Tis best,
This course. Our only one.—*Must* flood the
 mine.'

II

'Twas one short week since our brief rest
Was broken by a muffled roar,
A thund'rous mutter underground
In depths where Nature keeps a store
Of fiery force, close-pent and bound
In shining walls of brittle black,
For stalwart tools, with brawny might
Of Nature's higher force, to crack.

III

'Twas one short week since that glad night
When stalwart arms had dandled soft
The clinging brats, and tossed them high,
In rough farewell, o'er heads aloft :

Gurgling, gleeful, like to cry
To find their tiny heads so near
The rafters, and so far above
The mother's breast which is so dear
When dad's strong arms and dad's strong love
Are set to harder play than this.

IV

But one short week! Alas! how long!
What centuries seem fled! That kiss!
The last that father pressed upon
The mother-lips—now dumb and set,
Poor widowed lips! They nevermore
Will clack, nor gibe, nor idly fret
The strong, rough mate, who patient bore
The gibes and frets and idle clack;
—Or, may be, silenced all by times
With strong, rough word, or sounding whack
Of strong, rough fist, which ever grimes
More than it hurts alike the whacked
And whacker, did they read it right!

V

Seven long-drawn days of silence, racked
With torturing fear of what dread sight
May meet the dry, hot eyes that shrink,

There, at the pit-mouth, when each load
Of human ore comes to the brink,
Dug from the depths and thence bestowed
On eager hands for bearing home.

VI

—Or giving back to earth, may be,
With prayer and tears, 'neath Heaven's blue dome
High-arching, vast, serene : while we
Tóil, rage, weep, lay our dead to rest ;
And seldom raise a toil-worn front,
To drink draughts, sweet, reviving, blest,
From its pure fount ; but bear the brunt
Of sordid work with earth-fed strength,
With surly, doggèd, earth-born will ;
Until we lose both will and strength,
And lay us down—limbs stiff and still—
And leave our task to suppler hands.

. . . . . .

VII

For one brave week the rescuers wrought,
Undaunted, single-hearted bands !
Bold, eager toilers, who aid brought,
And hope, and longed-for gleams of light
To shattered limb and fainting heart
And straining eye.

VIII

              And though, in Sight
—For some—Hope now was lost ; and hearts,
Once faint, were now with God, and strong
For ever !—on the rescuers worked
Their painful way ; nor deemed it long,
Nor recked their lives, nor ever shirked
The cruellest task.
                  But smoke and stench
Tell tale of fire beyond,—and e'en
The boldest, bravest, can but blench
When fire's fell barrier flames between
His goal and him.
                And so—'twas o'er.

IX

' The missing, sure, cannot yet live.
' The dead lie quiet, and nevermore
' Will dread the scorching fate.
                      Come ! give
' The vain search o'er. Come ! Close the shaft.'
Thus went the master's word.
                        And then :
' Must flood the mine ; for mortal craft
' Nought else remains.'

X

    And now, rough men,—
Great giants whose coal-grit-grimed skin
Oft hides soft, tender, melting hearts,—
Came pleading if they might yet win
A passage through the smoke that parts
The horses, snorting, trembling brutes,
From upper air and safety.

XI
        ' No.
' One collier is worth myriad brutes.
' 'Twere madness ! '
       ' Measter ! let us go.
' The beasts will burn. Nay, let us down.'
' No. Never. They 're but brutes. They end
' In death. No ! ye shall not go down.'

XII

Thus Common Sense, plain, hard, doth lend
His sister, Sentiment, his strength
To keep her in due bound.
        But stay,—
Is Common Sense to run the length
Of gauging, meting out God's way

As to the Future for God's brutes?
Why not a heaven for them? Like man,
They love, they do their duty.—Faithful mutes!
What more, save talking, does a man?

IN REMEMBRANCE

I

CALM, pure, serene,
She went her maiden way,
And ever kept the golden mean
'Twixt fire and ice on Life's highway.

II

Her clear, true eye
Was ever keen to note
The true and good in passers-by.
Sweet eyes! undimmed by beam or mote.

III

Her kindly hand
Was ever quick to aid
The weaker ones upright to stand,
To guide the erring ones who strayed.

IV

Ah! calm, brave front!
That made our pathway bright.
Strong hand! whose clasp was ever wont
To make our heaviest burden light.

V

Clear glance! whose shine
Warmed while it pierced us through.
Loyal heart! whose love seemed nigh divine,
Because all free from self, all true.

VI

We loved her well,
And did her homage too,
As to a Queen.   But none durst tell
To her a meaner love, though true.

VII

She soared above
All lowly, selfish aims.
And grovelling passion—earth-born love—
On her free spirit had no claims.

VIII

And yet she knew
Its power to raise, or weight
To crush; and ever deemed it true
And wise for weaker souls to mate,

IX

Who dared not wend,
As she, Life's ways alone;
As she, beneath Life's burden bend,
And carry others' with her own.

X

Oh! sweet spring flowers!
Oh! fresh May sward so green!
Oh! gentle, fruitful, pearly showers!
Come! deck a couch as for a queen,

XI

On which to lay
Her dear, still form to sleep.
For she hath closed her eyes to-day :
Her rest has come, so sweet, so deep.

XII

Life's load no more
Those willing hands will bear;
Life's pains, life's tasks, for her are o'er.
For her—And we—? Must leave her there.

ATHLETICS

Nothing is new under the sun:
Man has the old, old course to run,
Round and round on the beaten track,
Not for a moment the pace must slack.

Steady and even, slow and sure,
Eyes front—arms bent—lungs free—heart pure,
Mind calmly set on the work, he flies,
Unheeding the onlookers' shouts and cries.

Training and staying power, not speed,
Faith in the Judge—'tis all we need
For a glorious winning of Life's grand race,
—Its prize:—To see Truth face to face.

THREE CHAPTERS FROM THE BOOK OF THE WISDOM OF JACOB TEW

I.—ON RELIGION

I

Coorate's bin oop at Eabram's 'ouse,
　Top o' 'bonk be'ynd—
'Im as 'is wyfe 'as getten twins,
　Threay wakes this deay, A mynd;

II

Fur Eabram 'e coom struttin' 'ere,
　Lyke a' 'en as 'as leade two heggs;
Sezee, ' Oo 's gin meay twins, oo 'as.'
　('Im as is bowed i' 'legs,

III

Odd mon oop 'th' faarm oop bonk.)
　Aa.　Eabram Baskervyle—?
Lyke as not 'is neam 's a-thattens,
　'Is muther wur theer awhyle.

IV

Well-well—Ee's dyedd, Owd Baskervyle—
   Ee's dyedd.—As A wur seay,
Coorate ee coom fur seay '*is* wyfe
   Abeout 'er choorchin' deay.

V

Eabram's wyfe's fur 'ave twins chrissened—
   Coorate an' 'er's that soart—
Hallweays fur choorch, oo is, hallweays—
   Coorate-mad—*that* soart.

VI

Sez-A,—Eabram's self wur chrissened
   An' yo an' meay, an-all.
A niver seay as it meade no differ
   'Twixt us an' Joshuay Ball.

VII

Ee niver 'ad no chrissenins,
   An' ee wur as owd as meay.
Nor A niver see 'im but twyct i' choorch
   Fro's birth to 's berryin' deay.

VIII

An A 've bin sexton, mon and bye,
    Fur nygh on threescore year,
An A niver berryed a better mon
    Nor Joshuay, niver tha fear.

IX

Joshuay niver sed no one neay—
    Ee wur fond o 's mate an 's eale,
But ee 'd gin it yo an' meay, an-all,
    If ee 'd thowt as A 'd missed ov a maale.

X

Ee niver thowt nowt on pollytricks,
    Ee did 'is deay's-work ryght ;
Owd muther an' 'im war quoiet foake
    As 'ad a oop-'ill fyght.

XI

Oo kept 'er 'ouse as clane as *clane*,
    Oo mended an' meade fur 'im ;
Oo dollied an' weshed fro' morn to nyght,
    Oo kept ooself nate an' trim.

XII

Joshuay niver wur one fur words—
  Dades wur all 'is seay.
An' yo 'll go fur tell meay, as Joshuay Ball
  Wonnat *stond* i' 'Joodgment Deay!

XIII

Coorate, ee 's all fur goin' to choorch
  Twyct ov a Sunday, an-all.
Coorate, ee pleays 'im all the wake
  Wi' th' net, an' 'wench, an' 'ball!

XIV

Owd Rector an' meay is meates, an-all—
  Ee pcays meay lyke a mon;
Sixpence a tyme fur 's 8-o'clock bell,
  Fur ee sez as A 'm owd an' done.

XV

An' *thissuns*, 'hyghth ov two-pennorth ov brass,
  Lyke a little yong bantin-cock,
Ee tells meay ma dooty, an' praches meay sick,
  An' spakes ov we-all as *'is flock*.

XVI

Owd Rector, *ee* niver pleays wi' nets
    Thin th' last stroake ov th' bell,
Nor slatts 'is bat upo' th' vestry floor
    An' on wi' 's soorplice!
                    Well!

XVII

A 'm nygh woore-eout wi' ringin' bell
    Ov a summer's afternoon—
'*Im* an' 'is tennisses an' wake-deay preayers!—
    An' owd Rector, thissun's '*is* son!

XVIII

Tymes is, tymes wur; but lyfe's seame.
    Gin meay a mon as duz
An' *duz*; an' 'owds 'is clackin' nyse,
    'Owds na-mure to '*im* nor *uz*.

XIX

Lives neeborly an' peays 'is weay,
    Duz 'is deay's work lyke a mon:
Choorch, chrissenins, coorates—as yo plase!—
    Tinna them as *saaves* a mon.

II.—ON WOMEN

I

God bless thee, wi' tha rough black yead!
   Coom 'ere, an' set thee down.
Our Joesiph sed a many tyme
   Ee 'd seen thee i' th' town.

II

Ea, lad! Thee 's getten 'wyfe, oo sez—
   (Our Sally, wi' 'er clack)—
Well, well! 'Tis commin fate ov mon
   Thin now, to Adam, back.

III

Neay-neay! A 'se niver getten 'wyfe!
   Thee 'st sure ov that, fur-sure.
But, si'thee, tho' A 've had no wyfe,
   'Wur pleagued wi' wenches mure.
    . . . . . .

IV

A seen a wench—one tyme—an-all ;
  As nice a wench as *nyce.* . . .
Oo's under 'sod, lad.—Under 'sod. . . .
  A berried 'er.—Aa, oo wur nyce.
    .   .   .   .   .   .

V

Neay. A 'll na-mure wi' wenches.—Neay!
    .   .   .   .   .   .

  A 'se getten a wench fur clane.
'Tis a-thissens wi' th' rhoomatiz,
  Connot kape th' 'ouse clane.

VI

An' so —A 'se getten wench fur clane.
  A slip ov a lass, oo wur—
Thee 'd 'a thowt as lads 'ud 'a letten 'er be,
  Oo wur quoiet as niver wur.

VII

Tell-ee, wur fair thrutcht-oop wi' lads !
  They coom ov a noon an' nyght !
A 'se getten gun, an' A let fly,—
  Got shut ov lads, a' ryght !

VIII

A catcht un i' th' fut, A did. . . .
   Ee meade meay peay for 't, though !
Fyve shillin's down to Joodge-in-Coort !
   Got shut ov wench. A did *so*.

IX

If yo 'll believe, as 'ere A sit—
   Oo blubbed thin-oo wur sick.
Oo sed A 'd spyled 'er chance fur lyfe—
   That theer lad wur 'er pick.

X

Oo sed as ee 'd getten pleace oop th' 'All—
   A-summat i' th' 'ouse—
An' *neow*, ee 'd niver be good fur nowt
   But shippons an' tentin' cows.

XI

A 'se getten anuther wench fur clane,
   An owd-un—Mosson's h'aunt
('Im as berried 'is wyfe last year,
   Th' widow-man)—Jane Sant.

XII

Oo 'd nygh bin death ov meay, oo 'ad !
  A 'd summat coom, that bad—
Oo sed 'twur joodgmint ov God, oo sed,
  Fur flying gun at 'lad !

XIII

Oo meade meay bottle ov stuff, oo did
  (Messin' an' dewin' wi' sass !) ;
A niver did 'old wi' doctor-trash,
  An' A throw'd thissen i' th' ass.

XIV

Oo sed, it done meay dyell ov good—
  Oo thowt a 'd tookt it ! Hee ! hee !
Hee ! hee !—Throw'd it i' th' ass, spune an' all !
  An' niver let on. Hee ! hee !

XV

A 'se getten shut ov Mosson's h'aunt.
  Ee lad ! A wur fyne an' glad !
Thowt as oo 'd pisoned meay, A did,
  Fur A wur fyne an' bad.

XVI

A leay abed, nygh goin' on year.
   A wur goin' fur pop off, A thowt.
An' coorate, ee thowt seame, ee did;
   Ee sent, fur tent meay,—a *nowt*!

XVII

Coorate-mad! A wench a-thissens,
   Preayin' over th' pleace;
Oo groaned, oo clackt, fur 'saave ma sowl,'
   Oo sed A wur ' 'opeless caase.'

XVIII

Hee! hee! The 'ouse wur 's black 's ma shoe,
   Oo 's letten milk go sour,
Oo 's getten bread as sad as cleay,
   Oo 's prached an' preayed by th' hour!

XIX

Oo sez, ' Yo 'll none give ear to meay:
   Ave coorate, *do*,' oo sez, ' do ee neow.'
Sez-A, ' A 'll none 'ave *'im*,' A sez;
   ' A 'm thrutcht wi' clackin' neow.'

XX

Oo sed oo 'd fetch John Jones fur preay
  (John Jones! A Methody-rant!) :
Sez-A, ' If *'Im* as A 'm goin' *to*
  Connat saave meay—*John Jones shan't.*'

XXI

A 'se getten shut ov *'er*.   Ee, lad!
  Wenches *is nowt*,—is nowt.
Thee 's getten wyfe—Pooer lad!   Pooer lad!
  Thee 's brewed a browst fur drought!

XXII

A'm moythered fyne, ' Why wenches coomed?'
  Godamyghty known!
Ee putt that theer Adam-lad
  I' gyardin, wi' wench, alone.

XXIII

Ee myght 'a know'd, if Ee'd 'a thowt,
  Nowt but mischeef *could* coom.
Aa—Wenches is meade fur werrit Mon.
  Fur why?   Ee 'll tell—at 'Doom.

III.—ON POLITICS

I

Ee, lad! A 'se getten trate, this deay.
A 've bin oop Minshull-weay,
A 've seen both them theer candidates,
A 'eard them seay their seay.

II

Owd Joodge's son wur theer, an-all
('Is son, as meade meay peay)—
A yong poll-parrit ov a lad—
A 'se getten a *trate* this deay!

III

Yong Joodge, ee 's all fur pollytricks,
Grandowdmon, an-all!
'Ome-reule (fine stuff!), eight-hours deay,
Dom choorchansteate, an-all!

IV

A niver did 'old wi' pollytricks—
'Tis stuff as wonnot wesh.
Pollytrickuns is thrutcht wi' words—
Lyke mugs-full ov wake bran mesh!

V

A sup ov *thattens* ov a nyght,
Wi' watter out-on a can!
Pig-wesh o' words! Tell ee, wi' that
Tha 'lt niver feed a *man*.

VI

Then Dutton oops an' 'as 'is seay.
Dutton 's mon fur meay!
Dutton, ee peays top pryce i' weage,
Dutton, *ee* 'll gain th' deay.

VII

Neay, neay, A 'm not goin' fur blab
'Is name as A ballits *fur*.—
Whatten soart wur Dutton lyke?—
A niver thowt *whatten* ee wur.

VIII

'Ast iver seen a moonkey, lad?
　Ee's summat that-a-weay.
'Tis brass as ee peays A 'old wi' un fur—
　Tinna looks as gains the deay.

IX

A 'olds wi' weage, *good brass*, an-all,
　An' A 'olds with a sup ov eale,
An' a summat i' th' Bonk, meay be,
　As 'll gin meay mate an' maale.

X

Squoires an' Passons, as yo plase—
　A 'll niver seay none-on-'em neay.
But 'old wi' Pollytricks—A wonnot!
　Tinna them as 'll gain the deay.

IN THE WAITING-ROOM OF AN EYE HOSPITAL

I

A GRIM, drab hall, with benches lined,
Where, ranged in dingy, shabby rows,
A patient crowd of human woes
Is waiting for relief.
     Blind! Blind!
The very walls might weep, had they a mind
For pity, and cry out,
      Sight for the blind!

II

Poor darkened ones, who dumbly plead
With upturned faces, in their night
Which is our day, so full, so bright—
Our working day for those who need
That we who see, to them in very deed,
Be eyes and hands, not only hearts that bleed.

III

These hard stone walls, were they not dumb,
These hard stone walls, begrimed with smoke,
Might tell a tale that strong men choke
With tears to hear the like ! The sum
Of pain and sorrow that they've seen would come
Far past all mortal reckoning. But they're dumb.

IV

Oh, ye with eyes to see !—The blind
For whom hearts bleed and stone walls weep,
They are not alway those who creep
And grope, their painful way to find
By touch and scent. No. There's a sadder kind
Of sightlessness—a grovelling, darkened mind,

V

That needs a glass to magnify
My Neighbour and diminish Me—
That needs a sharp, swift cut to free
The sick, dim-sighted mental eye
From blearing film of Self.
    Alas ! the I, Mine, Me,
    Unholy Idol Trinity !

VI

The prostrate masses it has crushed,
Its worshippers, makes Juggernaut
Seem kind !
        Self's creed is all untaught :
It needs no words by reverence hushed,
No music's thrill, no priceless glass rose-flushed,
No lofty sculptured fane.
                     Fount-wise, it gushed.

VII

Primeval, in primeval breast,
Each for himself the brutes began
The fight for life.
            But 'tis on Man
(Nay, 'tis on Woman, whose behest
The Man, poor fool, obeyed) the blame shall rest,
For madly, blindly, daring to invest

VIII

God's image in God's glory.
                       Yea,
Blind mother Eve, she moulded us
Our first false god. She, hoping thus

Her sons would godlike be.
                              That day
Arose an idol cult whose earthly sway
Is Catholic indeed !
                        Men bend and pray

IX

Before the great god Self, and bless
Jehovah, Allah, God, and Budh
('Soever be their Source of Good);
The same hands reverently dress
Two several altars ; and, devout, express
By folded palms obedience none the less

X

To one or t'other Power !—Blind ! blind !
This inward blindness causes all
These outward ills Eve's sons do call
Disease, vice, folly, crime !
                            Behind
The big-writ, sounding names we ever find,
Small-writ, the coward, lurking Self enshrined.
   .   .   .   .

XI

Ah, thou ! poor sufferer in yon hall !
Self's victim, immolated by

Thy own or others' haste to lie
Beneath the chariot wheel ! To fall,
And reck not, in the ecstasy, of all
Thy mad devotion brings ! Alas ! To enthrall

XII

Thyself—perchance thy farthest son ?—
Life-slave for one brief moment's bliss !
To seek to gain heav'n by one kiss !
To sip Self's loving-cup !—Nay, one
Sweet sip—but one poor taste !
                      Blind, blind, undone !
The kiss opes wide the gates of hell,—cheap
    won !

XIII

The sip brings death, or swift or slow,
Death to thyself and thine.
                      Widespread
The train of selfish joy ! The red,
Blood-red, and purple-shame-shot glow
That lights Self's dalliant path should serve to
    show
The flower-strown pitfalls, brimmed with miry
    slough,

XIV

That whelm the unwary,—did not we
Pursue our path with eyes blindfold!
Ye sad ones in yon hall, blindfold
With healing bands, that ye may see
Once more the light of day, tho' it may be
A day all-shadowed by your past.—
                              Ah me!

XV

Whose day is bright thro' all its course?—
To ye, from half-oped door, there sounds
Hope's voice. The surgeon on his rounds
With cheery tone brings taught resource
In skilful hands, to free you from the curse
Laid on you by the cruel darkening force

XVI

Ye dared, or worshipped, in the past,
—Ye, or your fathers!
                       Evermore,
For us, the blind who see, an opening Door
Brings Hope. There, voices from the Vast,
Strong, pure, resound. Gleams golden, cast
Like arrows, deal the death to Night.
                                At last

XVII

To blindness, self-love, sin, and woe
Will come a Knife, a Healer's skill;
And blindness, woe, and every ill
Will be removed for ever! Lo!
He comes! The door is widening! To and fro
Pass angels leading in the freed ones! Lo!
The Day beyond is brightening! Soon our night,
Our outer darkness, will be lost in Light!

BLUE HYACINTHS

I

BLUE hyacinths, from scented woods in spring!
Picked for loved hands by far-off loving hands,
And sent across the wide blue sea, to bring
The voiceless words that parted love demands.

II

Blue hyacinths from scented woods in spring!
Far off in years—so far, that Mem'ry faint
Calls Love to lend his plumy, untired wing
That she may fly to them thro' years, and paint
In veilèd blue, like Love's own eyes, their sweet,
Soft carpet, 'neath the tender shade of trees,
Scant-clothed in budding verdure, tipt by fleet,
Short sunbeams of the early year.

III

A breeze,
A waft of long-past, longed-for native air
Now fills with full, fresh life and force my frame,

—Tired with the gath'ring load of pain and care
Long years have brought, with lessening strength.—·
                    It came,
Free from the Source of Light and Love, that sent
The loving thought to pluck these flowers, that I,
Revived, might joy, and breathe their perfume, blent
With sweets from dear old native woods, brought nigh
By blest remembrance ;—

                    IV

                    Breathe, and so work on
With freshened power, and bear a lightened load,
Heartened once more and full of Hope ;
                        On, on,
Unflagging, driven by a flow'r-twinèd goad
Whose prick wounds not, and yet is strong to raise
My drooping energy, by thoughts it brings
Of youthful goals as yet ungained, of vows
Long-pledged, not yet fulfilled.

                    V

                    And most thought clings
To memories of one long gone to rest,
By whom my young, uncertain feet were led
To wander in the od'rous woods thus blest

For ever, to my heart, by her blest tread.—
The perfume of her life yet lives in hearts
Made sweet by loving her !

VI

       My life's true friend !
Albeit for me you bore no mother-smarts,
No pangs and throes—you bore the pangs that tend
To bring young souls to Life.
        The throes and hurts
That they, unknowing, cause to fost'ring guides
Who watch the advent, and whose care averts
The evil which the nascent soul betides.

VII

My tender guide ! Altho' I gave you pain,
I *know* you knew I loved you : by the trust
I place in all these heedless ones who pain
And wound me now ; yet, love me while they thrust.
For every pang I caused you, I have bled
In spirit since—perchance felt more than you !
For, ever in your breast sweet Mercy, wed
To lily-sceptred Patience, bred anew
Each day the God-like grace that pardons *all*.

VIII

My more than mother! I can ne'er forgive
My youth for hurting you. E'en now, the thrall
Of long-past sins lies on me, and I live
A life-long servant to Remorse, whose lash
Stings keen. Nor Penitence nor yet reform
Can reach you there, from me! I gnash
Blunt teeth in darkness, 'mid a wailing storm
Of griefs, raised all by my mad, youthful will!
And you? Do you float there above, serene,
With not one thought of me? Ah, no—for still
You love and pardon. From your heav'n you lean,
A 'blessèd damozel,' from out your bliss,
To gaze on me and lure me with sweet eyes,
Up from my dark, low place, that I may kiss
His feet, Whose pardoning Voice bids me arise

THE FIRST KISS

I

The meeting of two mouths!
The act man calls a kiss!
What is it makes for bliss
In meeting of two mouths?

II

Whence came it primal man
Devised this perfect art,
Whereby two souls apart
May bridge the awful span

III

That chasms One from One
By joining at the lip—
Whereby two souls may slip
Together, and make one?

IV

Ah! may it well have been
   When She, in Paradise,
   Stung on a sudden wise
(That awful span first seen),

V

Fled, terrorised, to Him,
   To still her heart's wild beat;
   And crouching at his feet,
Beset by fears, strange, dim,—

VI

Fear of this unknown mate—
   Her own who seemed to be—
   Unquestioned all, as she,
Till she aspiring ate,

VII

And tasted, with The Fruit,
   The acrid sap of doubt!—
   Then—her fair locks about
His path to stay his foot—

VIII

He, wondering, bent low
   To raise her to his breast;
   Her chill dread soothed to rest
Against his warm heart's glow:

IX

Then, seeing on her lip
   The fell fruit's poison-stain,
   Wild with despairing pain
Lest she die first—his lip

X

Pressed hers and drank death-dew
   To die with her. The pang
   Fired Love, and Hope upsprang
And Life was lit anew!

XI

For Love Immortal saw
   This mortal first-love kiss,
   And fused it with Love's bliss,
And sealed it as Love's Law.

'WORK—WHILE IT IS DAY.'

I

Why need we solve enigmas?
     Let us live!
Life is yet Life—Death, Death—
      When all is said.
The grain and chaff Time winnows in his sieve:
By winds of Circumstance the chaff is sped

II

The grain stays, to be set a-field, to grow.
The chaff is trodden in the mire, forgot;
The grain is—aught? Yea.—Why?
        We do not know
The chaff is—naught?
      Oblivion is *its* lot.

III

The golden grain encasquets deathless germs;
From one spring millions. Whenceforth?
      Who can tell?
The sagest husbandman, he naught affirms,
He ploughs, sows, reaps: And—
      All is well.

www.ingramcontent.com/pod-product-compliance
Lightning Source LLC
Chambersburg PA
CBHW031333160426
43196CB00007B/673